champagne

and sparkling wine

champagne

and sparkling wine

DISCOVERING ★ EXPLORING ★ ENJOYING

RYLAND
PETERS
& SMALL

LONDON NEW YORK

FIONA BECKETT

DESIGNER Pamela Daniels
EDITOR Sharon Ashman
PICTURE RESEARCH Emily Westlake
PRODUCTION Deborah Wehner
ART DIRECTOR Gabriella Le Grazie
PUBLISHING DIRECTOR Alison Starling

First published in the United States in 2004
by Ryland Peters & Small, Inc.
519 Broadway, 5th Floor
New York, NY 10012
www.rylandpeters.com

10 9 8 7 6 5 4 3 2 1

Library of Congress Cataloging-in-Publication Data

Beckett, Fiona.
  Champagne and sparkling wine : discovering,
exploring, enjoying / Fiona Beckett.-- 1st U.S. ed.
    p. cm.
  Includes index.
  ISBN 1-84172-697-4
  1. Champagne (Wine) 2. Sparkling wines. I. Title.
TP555.B45 2004
641.2'224--dc22
                                        2004006124

Printed in China

contents

★ DISCOVERING

★ EXPLORING

★ ENJOYING

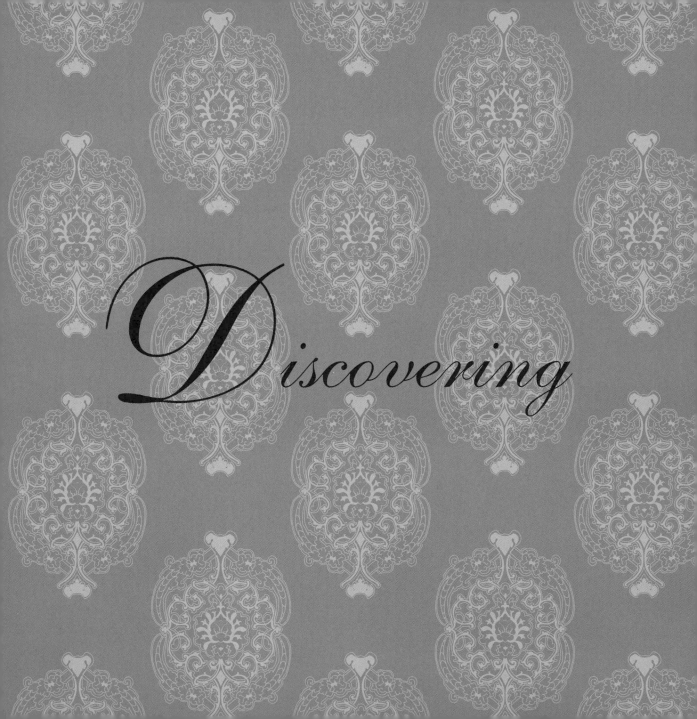

Discovering

You might think that champagne doesn't need discovering. After all, it is the most famous wine in the world. Yet we still tend to treat it as if it were a big brand like Coca-Cola® rather than one of the most complex and delightful styles of wine you can drink.

In fact, nowadays there is an amazing diversity of sparkling wine styles: bone dry or lusciously sweet. Fresh and fruity or mature and honeyed. White, pink, or red. From countries as far apart as Spain and New Zealand, there's a sparkling wine to suit every pocket and every occasion.

We might think we know this most celebratory of drinks, but there are lots of fascinating facts to discover. Did you know, for example, that a great deal of sparkling wine is made from dark-skinned grapes that are normally used for making red wine? That *brut* (dry) styles contain sugar? Or that champagne's bubbles are merely trapped carbon dioxide? You didn't? Intrigued? Then read on . . .

how sparkling wines get their sparkle

If you tasted champagne before it got its bubbles, you wouldn't like it. It's a miracle how the undistinguished, still, thin, sharp wine that forms the base of the most famous fizz in the world is transformed into an elegant drink that is synonymous with glamour and excitement.

Sparkling wine is made by converting a low-alcohol base wine, sugar, and yeast into alcohol and carbonic gas. In the case of champagne and other top-quality sparkling wines, this process takes place in the bottle so that the carbon dioxide that is released by the process is trapped and turns into bubbles. With cheaper fizz this secondary fermentation generally takes place in a tank (like many still wines), in a combination of bottles and tanks, or simply by injecting carbon dioxide into the wine just like you would to make a seltzer.

Although it is widely believed that the French invented champagne, it was in fact the English who, in the seventeenth century, first accepted sparkling wine as a desirable drink rather than merely an unfortunate accident. It was they who also developed the specially strengthened bottles needed to prevent champagne from exploding. However, it was undoubtedly the French who developed the techniques that made champagne marketable. The art of blending different wines and of making a light wine from dark-skinned grapes is credited to the monk Dom Pérignon, of the Abbey of Hautvillers outside Epernay, whose name lives on in one of the most famous prestige cuvées. And it was the young widow of an early champagne producer, Veuve Clicquot, who discovered the practice of turning the bottles regularly to dislodge the sediment left over from fermentation (page 15), and thus enabling a clear wine to be made.

In the second half of the 19th century, the invention of machines and techniques for rapidly ejecting the sediment and topping up bottles with reserve wine and sugar, meant it was possible to make champagne on a vast scale. Thirty million bottles a year were being produced by the end of the 1890s when it was—and has since remained—the world's most fashionable drink.

WHY THEY TASTE SO DIFFERENT

If the method of making sparkling wines is broadly similar, why do they taste so different to each other? There are a number of reasons for this.

★ **CLIMATE** Grapes grown for sparkling wine in hot climates, such as Australia, produce wines with a fuller flavor, but which lack the longevity of wines from cooler regions like Champagne.

★ **SOIL** Few parts of the world have the distinctive chalky soils of the Champagne region, which adds hugely to champagne's finesse.

★ **THE VARIETY AND QUALITY OF GRAPES USED** The classic champagne grapes are Chardonnay, which contributes elegance and freshness, Pinot Noir, which gives body and depth, and Pinot Meunier, which adds fruitiness and roundness. A sparkling wine will taste different depending upon which of these grapes predominates, or whether other grapes such as Chenin Blanc, Pinot Blanc, or Riesling are used. Muscat for example, the grape that is used to make Asti, makes an exotically grapey wine, nothing like champagne. Sparkling Shiraz is also vastly different. But even if you use the classic grapes, you can't turn them into fantastic fizz unless they are grown specially for the purpose of making sparkling wine, otherwise they can get overripe, resulting in a wine that is too high in alcohol and not at all refreshing.

★ **HOW MUCH FIZZ THERE IS** That is to say how much carbonic gas has dissolved in the wine. Some wines, such as the Portuguese vinho verde, have merely a prickle, some like Moscato d'Asti are gently sparkling, while most champagnes have a vigorous mousse.

★ **HOW MUCH SUGAR IS ADDED** With the exception of a very few *brut nature* champagnes, most sparkling wines have a little sugar added to prevent them tasting too sharp. The amount of sugar can vary between *brut*, which tastes completely dry and *demi-sec* or *halb-trocken* styles, which taste quite sweet (page 35).

★ **HOW LONG THEY ARE AGED** Some wines, like Moscato d'Asti, are meant to be drunk young and fresh. Others, such as vintage champagne, need several years to develop their rich, toasty flavor (page 17). We consumers also play our part with regard to how long we keep it and how we store it.

★ **SKILL AND EXPERIENCE** Here, the Champagne producers have the edge. After all, they have been making it for three centuries compared to the mere three decades of many New World producers. But the dividing line between champagne and other top sparkling wines is breaking down fast, not least because many of the champagne houses have become involved with wineries in the New World. Where Champagne is still unrivaled is in its quality and diversity of raw materials, including older wines from previous vintages, and its skill in blending them.

champagne

Drive through Champagne and you'll see nothing dramatic in the way of scenery. Despite the fact that the heart of the region is known as La Montagne de Reims, it's hilly rather than mountainous, with the pretty, gently rolling slopes making way for the plains that were the tragic site of some of the most bitter battles of the First World War. Only the palatial headquarters of champagne houses in Reims and Epernay tell you that this is home to the most luxurious and celebrated of drinks.

What makes champagne so special is the famous French concept of *terroir*. The region—just 90 miles (145 km) northeast of Paris—is extraordinarily far north for grape growing, but nevertheless has a climate in which the classic sparkling wine grapes of Chardonnay, Pinot Noir, and Pinot Meunier achieve their finest expression. The cool conditions intensify their flavor while preserving their acidity and freshness. Cool, damp, dark cellars, some of them many hundreds of years old, preserve those qualities. Above all, there's the distinctive chalky soil, conserving moisture for the vines and giving its special, elegant mineral character to the grapes.

Like winegrowers in many other areas of France, the Champenois, as the growers and producers are called, have been making wine for generations. So intimately do they know every inch of their vineyards that they can make a completely different champagne from grapes that are picked within a few yards of each other. That's what makes this drink so special.

HOW THE CHAMPAGNE REGION IS ORGANIZED

Everything in Champagne is expensive: the labor, because the grapes are harvested by hand; the land, with some of the most expensive vineyards in the world; and the grapes, which cost as much as table grapes. The huge cost of keeping older stocks of wine, expensive advertising, and not least, the palatial headquarters of the champagne houses, make it easy to see why the cost of champagne is as high as it is.

What's fascinating, however, is that behind all the glamour is a huge agricultural enterprise relying on thousands of small growers (over 19,000 at the latest count), many of whom have just a hectare or two of land. These small growers produce the variety of grapes needed by the big champagne producers to create complex wines. These smallholdings are found all over the region—from just above Reims to the north, right down to the Aube, southeast of Troyes, in the south.

Some areas are famous for particular grapes. The Côte des Blancs, for example, is renowned for its Chardonnay, while some of the best Pinot Noir comes from the Montagne de Reims.

The 17 most highly rated villages are officially classified as Grand Cru and only produce Chardonnay and Pinot Noir, not the lesser rated (though hugely important) Pinot Meunier. There are also 43 villages classified as Premier Cru, which account for just under a quarter of all champagne production. Some villages have vineyards that qualify as both Grand and Premier Cru for different grape varieties.

However, there is also a significant amount of champagne that does not have a famous name attached to it. A great deal is produced by co-operatives (associations of growers) and individual winemakers who grow their own grapes. There are, therefore, thousands of different brands, many marketed under their own label by wine merchants, supermarkets, and restaurants.

HOW NON-VINTAGE CHAMPAGNE IS MADE

When it comes to making sparkling wine, the champagne method—also referred to as the *méthode champenoise* and *méthode traditionelle*—is regarded as the model. In essence, this method is about letting the second fermentation—the process of converting yeast and sugar into alcohol and bubbles— take place in the bottle. But the way champagne is made involves other distinctive features that differentiate it from conventional winemaking.

First, all the harvesting is done by hand to avoid crushing the grapes. The grapes are then pressed very gently so that the juice doesn't pick up any color from the skins of the darker grapes. Each batch of juice is kept in separate tanks and fermented to an alcoholic strength of 10.5 to 11 percent. This normally takes place in stainless steel tanks, although some producers use large oak casks as well.

In the spring following the harvest, samples are taken from all the different batches to make the final blend of wine (the *assemblage*). This may include up to 40 or 50 components as well as wines from previous vintages, the skill being to create a sparkling wine that follows a consistent house style. Red wine may be added to produce a rosé champagne.

A solution of yeast, sugar, and wine is then added and the resulting wine is put into reinforced bottles, sealed with a crown cap, and left to ferment again.

After the second fermentation has taken place, the wine lies undisturbed in deep, dark cellars for a minimum of 15 months, but more usually between 18 months and three years. By this stage the yeast has ceased to be active but its residue (the lees) imparts a rich creamy flavor.

In order to clarify the wine, this sediment needs to be removed. The bottles are gradually shaken and upended so that the sediment moves down to the neck of the bottle. This process—referred to as riddling—used to be carried out by hand in specially angled wooden racks and took about two months to complete. Nowadays, the same result can be achieved by a machine in just over a week, although the most expensive champagnes are still handled in the traditional way.

The neck of the bottle is dipped into a freezing solution to solidify the yeast residue, which is then forcibly ejected or "disgorged." The bottle is topped up with a wine and sugar solution (the *dosage*) which varies depending upon how sweet a style is desired. It is then sealed with the distinctive champagne cork and secured with a wire muzzle. Most quality producers will let the champagne mature for an additional three to six months before it is labeled and released.

VINTAGE AND NON-VINTAGE CHAMPAGNE

The difference between vintage and non-vintage champagne sounds like a choice between good and less good fizz, but it's not that simple.

Officially, non-vintage champagne can't be released until it is 15 months old, but many producers hold onto theirs for as long as three to four years. The age of the individual wines in the blend can also vary from as little as 5 percent of wine from the previous year, to as much as 50 percent of wine from the last six years, so some wines taste very much lighter (and occasionally sharper) than others.

The situation is similar with vintage champagne, which must be made entirely from grapes from a single vintage (i.e., harvest), as opposed to some vintage sparkling wines, which can be made from a minimum of 85 percent of grapes from one harvest. Vintage bottles of fizz must be no less than three years old when released, but they are often not put on the market until they are five or six years old.

There's a special category of very expensive vintage fizz which is kept on its lees even longer, then disgorged (page 15) just before it is released, the most famous example being Bollinger RD (*récemment dégorgé*). Even if they are very old, these wines have a surprising freshness, but lack the staying power of wines that have been bottled earlier. Not that you're likely to worry about that if you get your hands on one; most of us would drink it rather than keep it!

★ WHAT ARE THE BEST VINTAGES?

IN THEORY, VINTAGE CHAMPAGNES ARE ONLY RELEASED IN EXCEPTIONAL YEARS, WHICH WOULD AMOUNT TO TWO OR THREE YEARS OUT OF EVERY TEN. IN PRACTICE, PRODUCERS ALSO TEND TO RELEASE VINTAGE CHAMPAGNES IN YEARS THAT ARE ABOVE AVERAGE, BRINGING THE TOTAL TO ABOUT FOUR OR FIVE A DECADE. THE BEST VINTAGES OVER THE LAST FEW DECADES HAVE BEEN:

2002 (NOT DUE TO BE RELEASED UNTIL 2007/8)
1999
1998
1996
1995
1990
1989
1988
1985
1982

the rest of france

Why would you drink a French sparkling wine that wasn't champagne? Well, for the same reason that you might drink any other fizz—because it was less expensive (particularly if you were buying it on the spot) and offered a different spectrum of flavors.

Most French wine-producing regions have their own fizz which, with one or two exceptions, is mainly for local consumption. The description *crémant* is increasingly replacing the confusing selection of names under which these wines used to be known, such as *mousseux* and *pétillant*. It indicates a wine of higher than average quality made by the traditional champagne method and often includes a significant proportion of Chardonnay, though a variety of other grapes are used, too.

The Loire region is one of the most important sparkling wine-producing areas of France. Its crisp, dry wines are mainly based on Chenin Blanc—well-known appellations are Saumur, Vouvray, and Crémant de Loire. There is also a fair amount of sparkling wine in Alsace (Crémant d'Alsace) and Burgundy (Crémant de Bourgogne), neither area far from the Champagne region.

Further south, the most interesting fizz comes from around the Languedoc town of Limoux, which also lays claim to having produced the first sparkling wine in France. The appealing apple-flavored Blanquette de Limoux, based on the local Mauzac grape, now competes with the more contemporary Crémant de Limoux, which includes a higher proportion of Chardonnay. Dry sparkling wine is also made in Gaillac, Jura, and Savoie, but this rarely makes it to the export market.

italy

Italy's best known sparkling wines are as distinctive as its still ones. The most popular is the increasingly fashionable Prosecco—the base for the bellini cocktail and the staple drink of Venetians. Generally, the wines are simple and soft, though high-quality ones are made around Valdobbiádene. The best, from producers such as Bisol and Col Vetoraz, are made from grapes grown on the dramatic hillside vineyards of Cartizze.

In Piedmont to the west are the vineyards of Asti (formerly Asti *spumante*) and the rather more reliable Moscato d'Asti, a delectably grapey, light, honeysuckle-sweet wine made from Muscat grapes. At just 5 percent alcohol, it's the perfect summer fizz.

Finally, there is Lambrusco. Not the vapid, over-sugared horror of a few years ago, but a bitter-sweet, cherry-flavored red that cuts through the local pork dishes of Emiglia Romagna beautifully. Noted producers are Bellei, Chiarli, and Corte Manzini.

More conventional sparkling wines based on the classic champagne grapes can be found in the Franciacorta region to the east of Milan.

Spain has hit the jackpot with its hugely successful cava—one of the best-priced sparkling wines available today. Made just to the north of Barcelona, its costs are kept down by highly efficient, modern methods of production and by the use of the inexpensive, high-yielding local grape varieties Parellada, Macabeo, and Xarel-lo.

Basic cava used to be very dry and yeasty, but the addition of increasing amounts of Chardonnay have created a pleasant, vanilla-flavored fizz that makes a great base for cocktails. There is also a strawberry-flavored cava rosado and vintage (*reserva*) cava, which has a more pronounced yeasty, toasty character, more akin to older champagne.

The two industry giants are Codorníu and Freixenet, which bottles its Cordon Negro in distinctive black bottles.

spain

england

With almost exactly the same soil and climate as the north of the Champagne region, it's not surprising that the south of England produces world-class sparkling wines that are uncannily similar to the real thing. The only factors that stop it being more successful are the cost (it's not much cheaper than champagne) and the limited volumes that are produced. Top growers include Nyetimber, RidgeView, and Valley Vineyards in Berkshire.

23

germany

Despite the popularity of sparkling wines among Germans—whose two biggest producers actually make more fizz than the whole of the Champagne region—their own Sekt was relatively undistinguished until a few years ago, with a considerable proportion of it being made from imported wine.

As in other parts of the world though, quality has improved significantly. Although most Germans still buy big brands such as Deinhard, Faber, and Sohnlein, the most interesting wines tend to come from small producers, particularly those that are made from Germany's most distinguished grape variety, Riesling. There are also some fine rosé sparkling wines made from Pinot Noir grapes, which are known as Spätburgunder in Germany.

Look for the description Deutscher Sekt, which means that the wine is produced exclusively from grapes grown in Germany. Wines that come from a specific region or vineyard are labeled Sekt bA.

the rest of europe

Some sparkling wine is produced almost everywhere in Europe where still wine is produced, especially in the central European countries of Austria, the Czech Republic, Hungary, Slovenia, and Switzerland. However, little of this gets exported. Portugal's vinho verde also has a natural spritz that just about takes it into the sparkling wine category.

Outside Champagne, northern California currently vies with New Zealand (page 27) as the world's best producer of sparkling wine—its cool, fog-cloaked coastline providing near-perfect growing conditions for the classic champagne grapes. Heavy investment by champagne houses such as Moët et Chandon (Domaine Chandon), Roederer, Mumm (Cuvée Napa), and the giant Spanish cava producers Freixenet (Gloria Ferrer) and Codorníu has led to a sophisticated market whose producers offer several styles of fizz.

In general, the wines are fuller in flavor than non-vintage champagne, with a softer, vanilla-scented edge or a rich, honeyed toastiness. Most are sold at reasonable prices, though top cuvées such as Domaine Carneros' Le Reve (owned by Taittinger), and Roederer's L'Ermitage deservedly fetch prices equivalent to vintage champagne.

California also has some of the world's best organized wine tourism, with many sparkling wine domaines offering excellent restaurants and tasting facilities. You can even get married in some of them! (Check their individual websites for details.)

Of the other US states—and many boast a couple of sparkling wine producers—Oregon shows the most promise with Argyle being its most well-known name. Canada also produces a fair quantity of sparkling wine, including some wonderfully exotic (and very pricey) sparkling ice wine.

north america

south america

South America's sparkling wine production hasn't kept pace with its reds or whites, but there is a modest amount of congenial fresh-tasting fizz in both Argentina and Chile. The giant Moët et Chandon group is involved in this part of the world, too, with their Domaine Chandon winery in Argentina. Valdivieso leads the field in Chile. Given South America's success in attracting consumers, it's probably only a matter of time before it cracks the sparkling wine market as well.

australia

Just as its Chardonnay has won the hearts of the world's consumers, so have Australia's easy, approachable, affordable, sparkling Chardonnay and soft strawberry-flavored rosés. But it is also producing some increasingly sophisticated, complex wines in cooler areas like the Yarra valley north of Melbourne and Tasmania (also wonderful areas to visit). Brands to look out for include Croser, Edwards and Chaffey, Green Point (made by the ubiquitous Moët et Chandon group), and Pipers Brook's Pirie from Tasmania.

Australia's unique contribution to the world of fizz, however, is its wonderfully frivolous sparkling red, initially based on Shiraz but nowadays made from Cabernet Sauvignon and even an obscure grape variety like Durif (by De Bortoli). Put champagne firmly out of your mind: this is a fantastic, full-throttle, fruity style that goes brilliantly well with a barbie.

new zealand

Such is the New Zealand wine industry's drive for perfection that they won't be content until their sparkling wines rival champagne. And it's a tribute to their biggest producer, Montana, that so many of their wines, sold under the Deutz and Lindauer labels, are not far from doing just that.

The Marlborough region in the north of the South Island undoubtedly has the right climate for quality sparkling wine production—it's just a question of time before their wines are counted among the world's best. Other names to look out for are Pelorus (made by the famous Cloudy Bay), Miru Miru, and Cellier Le Brun.

south africa

Even though their climate is on the warm side for producing sparkling wine, the seriousness with which South Africans take it is indicated by the fact that they have their own term for the champagne method, "cap classique." I can remember being seriously impressed when one of their more flamboyant winemakers, Achim von Arnim of Cabriere estate, took the top off a bottle with a saber. His Pierre Jourdan range is well worth trying, particularly the rosé. Look out, too, for fizz from Simonsig, Villiera, and the very reasonably priced wines from Graham Beck.

Exploring

As you become more familiar with sparkling wine, you discover what style you like, which won't necessarily be the most expensive bottles on the market. Everyone has a different palate: some enjoy the complex mushroomy flavors of old champagne, some would much rather have one that tastes fresh and lively, and still others look for one with a touch of strawberry fruit or honeysuckle sweetness.

The following pages reveal how—and where—to find them, what sort of sparkling wine to pick in a restaurant or wine bar or for a special occasion, and what you need to know in order to serve sparkling wine at its best. The ideal storage conditions, the most effective way of chilling a bottle (fast!), and the perfect glasses are also covered, as well as some hints on how to taste.

sparkling
wine styles

The Champenois (as the wine producers of Champagne are called) never tire of telling you that champagne is a wine. This is not just a line. In just the same way as a producer of still wines will create a range of wines from different grape varieties and at different prices, the typical producer of sparkling wines will produce several different cuvées (blends) that can differ quite markedly from each other in style.

★ HOW CHAMPAGNE USED TO TASTE

ALTHOUGH IT'S HARD TO IMAGINE, CHAMPAGNE WAS ORIGINALLY A STILL WINE AND IN THE 19TH CENTURY AND EARLY PART OF THE 20TH CENTURY, IT WAS MUCH SWEETER THAN IT IS NOW—MORE LIKE TODAY'S *DEMI-SEC*. IT OFTEN HAD BRANDY ADDED, TOO, WHICH MUST HAVE MADE IT TASTE MORE LIKE THE CLASSIC CHAMPAGNE COCKTAIL (PAGE 56).

LIGHT AND FRESH

This is a style most producers will have somewhere in their range—a refreshing, easy-drinking bottle of fizz that you can serve on its own without food. Typically, the predominant flavors will be fruity—citrus and apple with maybe a hint of peach and vanilla. Most inexpensive sparkling wines and non-vintage champagnes fall into this category, although those labeled Blanc de Noirs (page 34) may be more full-bodied.

There are also certain champagne houses or producers that are noted for making their non-vintage champagne in this style—Laurent Perrier, Perrier-Jouët, Pommery, and Taittinger, for instance—though they will become more weighty with age. In some cases their prestige cuvées also exhibit this character, especially if drunk young. Pommery's Cuvée Louise is one example.

Non-vintage champagne and sparkling wines made from Chardonnay alone, known as Blanc de Blancs, also tend to have a creamy vanilla edge that puts them firmly into the light-bodied camp, as do some French *crémant* wines (page 19) that include a smattering of Chardonnay. Bone-dry *ultra brut* or *extra brut* champagnes that have no added sugar are always light and elegant in style.

Finally, any dry white sparkling wine that is deliberately designed *not* to taste like champagne falls into this light and fresh category, for example wines made from aromatic grape varieties such as Riesling (like some Sekts) or Italy's most famous soft sparkler, Prosecco.

CLASSIC, MEDIUM-BODIED

These are wines that are deliberately made in a slightly fuller style or that have acquired some bottle age. They are generally a balanced blend of the classic champagne grape varieties rather than being made from just Chardonnay or dominated by dark-skinned Pinot Noir and Pinot Meunier. You may pick up notes of yeast, toast, and honey, although these flavors won't be as pronounced as they are in the full-bodied style (page 34).

Champagnes that fit this description include Moët et Chandon and Veuve Clicquot. Spanish cava is also traditionally made in this style although it is increasingly being made to taste lighter and creamier. English sparkling wine also echoes the champagne style as do some New Zealand sparkling wines like Lindauer and Pelorus, which exhibit a yeasty, biscuity character. They pair well with food, but are not quite as flexible in this respect as the full-bodied styles.

RICH AND FULL-BODIED

There are three main ways a champagne or sparkling wine becomes full-bodied. The first is the choice of grapes. Wines made from the dark-skinned grapes Pinot Noir and Pinot Meunier will generally taste fuller and richer than those made from Chardonnay or other white grapes. In Champagne, wines made with the darker-skinned grapes are called Blanc de Noirs.

The second is through age. The longer a wine spends on its lees (the yeast residues left over from fermentation, page 15), the more character it develops. The predominant flavors are toast, honey, and—over time—mushroom and truffle. Vintage champagnes tend to be full-bodied simply because of the amount of time they have spent in the cellars, although some vintages, such as 1990 and 1996, are richer than others.

The third way to achieve a full-bodied wine is through oak aging. Producers who ferment their wines in oak barrels like Alfred Gratien, Krug, and Vilmart all produce fuller-bodied wines than those who use stainless steel.

Just as some champagne houses consciously make their non-vintage wines in a lighter style, others such as Bollinger, Gosset, and Louis Roederer make theirs richer and more complex. Top sparkling wines from other New World producers such as Cellier Daniel Le Brun and Montana in New Zealand, and Domaine Chandon, Petaluma, and Seaview in Australia, are also heavyweight customers. Prestige cuvées like Dom Pérignon and Roederer's Cristal obviously come into this category, too, particularly their older vintages.

Wines like this are wasted on party drinking (unless you're a rock star) and are better saved for a special meal (see page 50 for food pairing ideas).

OLD AND MELLOW

I'm still talking about what's in the bottle here, not the people who drink it. However, it's true to say that this is a style of sparkling wine—and champagne in particular—that appeals to the aficionado with a deep pocket, and probably someone who's been drinking champagne all of his or her life.

They buy the best and deliberately allow it to age so that it develops the flavor of wild mushrooms and truffles and becomes the color of old gold. It's not to everyone's taste, but it is a piece of history. If somebody offers to share a bottle with you, grab the chance!

ROSÉ

Pink fizz sounds the most frivolous of wines but in the Champagne region they take it very seriously, releasing their most expensive prestige cuvées like Dom Pérignon, Krug, and Veuve Clicquot La Grande Dame in a rosé version. These are immensely rich, full-bodied wines that are intended to be aged for a decade or more and served with food—usually lamb or game, served rare, often with mushrooms or truffles to complement the mature, mushroomy flavors of the wine.

At the other end of the scale there are bright, light, strawberry-flavored sparklers that are fun and inexpensive such as Cava Rosado or Australian brands like Seaview. These are perfect for drinking on a picnic or a warm summer's evening.

What determines the style is how much contact the juice has had with the grape skins or how much red wine has been added. Add very little and you get an ethereally pale onion-skin pink that is weirdly referred to in France as *oeil de perdrix* (partridge's eye). Add more and you get a rich, almost cherry-colored wine that bursts with ripe summer fruits.

Most rosé champagne is somewhere between the two—prettily pink with delicate wild strawberry flavors, the ultimate choice for romantic occasions.

RED

Red sparklers (they don't make them in Champagne) are something of a rarity, but have a distinctive character. There are two main sources—the Emilia Romagna region of Italy, which produces bittersweet cherry-flavored Lambrusco, and Australia with its exuberant, sweet, juicy, sparkling Shiraz and Cabernet, which have become a habitual partner to the Aussie barbecue. They are also a fun Christmas or Thanksgiving wine— they go fantastically well with turkey!

SWEET

As with still dessert wines, when it comes to fizz there's sweet, and there's sweet. On the one hand, you will discover the off-dry, newly fashionable "rich" style, much favored by the Champenois for serving with foie gras. While on the other hand there's the delicate, honeysuckle sweetness of Italy's Moscato d'Asti or Clairette de Die Méthode Dioise, the muscat-based wine of the Rhône. The best known classification for sweet sparkling wine is *demi-sec*, but you will occasionally find such wines in other regions of France referred to as *moelleux*. Sweet fizz, like sweet wine, tends to be looked down upon, but while some bottlings can be coarse, the best can make an indulgent partner for cakes and summer fruits.

buying fizz

Although price is always a consideration when you are buying wine, it's even more critical when you are buying champagne. This is partly because it is an expensive drink and partly because if you're acquiring it for a party, wedding, or other large celebration, you will need to buy a lot of it.

The good news is that there are often deals available, particularly at peak buying periods such as on the run-up to Christmas, New Year, and Valentine's Day, so you rarely need to pay full price. However, you do need to be wary of bottles that are being sold at a suspiciously cheap price. Always try a bottle of a brand you've never come across before you splash out on a case. Be wary of older vintage champagnes (1990 or earlier) that may be past their best. Remember, too, that since sparkling wine is sensitive to light, avoid buying bottles that have been sitting in a window display or under hot spotlights.

Don't feel you have to go for famous names (unless impressing your friends is the main objective!). Some less well-known champagne labels from small growers may well be available from liquor stores or wine merchants. These are often carefully sourced and can be excellent value, compared to the big-brand names.

The other option is to buy direct from a producer, particularly if you live within reach of a sparkling wine-producing area. San Francisco, for instance, is just a few hours' drive from Napa Valley, where it's great fun to taste and buy at the cellar door.

WHAT SIZE TO BUY?

Champagne is bottled in an extraordinary range of sizes, from quarter bottles to the colossal Nebuchadnezzar—the equivalent of twenty 750 ml bottles. The biggest I would actually choose, and which you could realistically fit in your refrigerator, is a Jeroboam (the equivalent of four bottles), but magnums (two bottles) and half-bottles are more practical alternatives. Magnums are great for a dinner party, while half-bottles are perfect for a single person or a couple. Some producers such as Pommery also make dinky 200 ml bottles to be consumed with a straw!

ordering

sparkling wine

Ordering bubbly in a bar or a restaurant is not cheap. This is an item on which restaurants make their mark-up, particularly on well-known brands. The restaurant manager or sommelier's solicitous request as to whether you would like a glass of champagne, as if it were on the house, is not to make you feel pampered but rather to keep their bank manager happy.

If you enjoy a glass of sparkling wine as an aperitif—and it makes a very good one, by the way—ask for the wine list to check the price and also to see what other kinds of sparkling wine are available. In an Italian restaurant, for example, Prosecco is a much cheaper alternative.

As far as champagne is concerned, the best value is to be found in bars where the owner has a personal passion for fizz and a big selection to choose from. Alternatively, choose a restaurant that prides itself on locating good-quality wines generally, and takes pride in its house champagne.

If there are more than two of you, it may be cheaper to order by the bottle, especially in a restaurant. You can easily continue drinking bubbly through the first course.

in bars & restaurants

special occasions

So automatic is the association between celebrations and champagne that some people regard it as virtual heresy to consider anything else. But with the high quality of sparkling wine that's now being produced elsewhere in the world, there's no reason why you shouldn't consider an alternative to champagne. Personally, I'd much prefer a glass of good sparkling wine rather than a poor champagne anytime.

As with everything wine related, the type of sparkling wine you choose will depend on the occasion and your guests. For example, if you were giving a small lunch party for your parents' golden wedding anniversary, this would be a natural opportunity to serve something special like a vintage champagne, preferably in a magnum. On the other hand, the 100 or so twenty-somethings at your son or daughter's 21st birthday party might well prefer a much more economical sparkling Chardonnay. If you were treating your loved one to a special Valentine's Day dinner, you might want to make a romantic gesture and serve pink champagne. For a summer tea party to celebrate a christening, you could serve Prosecco.

If you're trying to keep costs down, there's nothing wrong with serving two different kinds of sparkling wine. For instance, at a wedding you could serve a stylish sparkling wine from New Zealand or California at the reception, and use champagne for the toasts. Or—rather more sneakily—you could kick off with a bottle that everyone will recognize, then switch to a less expensive one once your guests have reached the stage when they will no longer notice!

There's a lot to be said for creating an occasion spontaneously rather than planning ahead—take a bottle of bubbly on a picnic, for example, or pop a cork to celebrate a promotion, a new job, or unexpected good news like an engagement. Somehow anything other than champagne seems a bit half-hearted for these particular moments. Champagne is a celebration in itself.

storing fizz

Like most wines nowadays, the majority of sparkling wine is consumed within days, or at most weeks, of being bought. Unlike many wines, a sparkling wine is already mature when it is released. Most non-vintage champagnes have spent two to three years in a bottle, vintage champagnes double that time. Sparkling wines are similar: there's no advantage to keeping them for any length of time, particularly inexpensive bottles or ones that are designed to be drunk young, such as rosé and Moscato fizz. However, it is wise to leave any sparkling wine a couple of days to settle before drinking it in case it has been shaken up on the trip home.

That said, most bottles will keep perfectly well, and younger champagnes may even improve for six months to a year provided the storage conditions are right. Vintage champagnes have the ability to age a lot longer—up to 10 or 15 years from the harvest date—but you may not enjoy their slightly mushroomy, truffley flavors as much as the fresher fruit of a younger bottle. Vintage-dated New World sparkling wines tend to mature more rapidly and should generally be drunk within one to two years of purchase.

The ideal conditions for storing fizz are the same as for still wine—a cool, dark space with a constant temperature of around 57–59°F (14–15°C). That's not easy in today's constantly heated homes, but if you can at least ensure the temperature doesn't fluctuate too violently, your bottles should be reasonably happy. Sparkling wine will keep well stored upright (the carbon dioxide in the bottle keeps the cork moist), but old habits die hard and most people store it horizontally like other wines.

Leftover champagne will retain its fizz for two to three days in the refrigerator if you seal the bottle with a sparkling wine stopper. However, don't leave unopened bottles in the fridge for any length of time—this over-chills them and can extract moisture from the cork, letting air in.

serving fizz

To enjoy champagne or sparkling wine at its best you need to chill it—not just for the taste, but to preserve the bubbles and to stop the cork popping out too quickly when you open the bottle. Don't over-chill it, however, or you will destroy the subtle nuances of flavor in the wine. For most sparkling wines, one and a half hours in the refrigerator should be just about right. Vintage champagne needs slightly less time.

Quicker methods of chilling include plunging the bottle into a bucket of water and ice cubes or popping it in the freezer for 15 minutes, but for goodness' sake, don't forget you've put it there or the bottle may explode! You can also buy purpose-made insulated jackets that can be frozen and slipped over the bottle, but tip the bottle gently from side to side to ensure the contents are evenly chilled before opening it.

To open a bottle, tear off the foil, unwind the twisted piece of wire that holds the cork in place, and remove the wire cap. Holding the top end of the bottle in your left hand with your thumb over the cork, twist the base of the bottle with your right hand (vice versa if you're left-handed) until you begin to feel the cork ease out. Keep holding

onto the cork lightly and let the pressure in the bottle force it out. It should emerge with a quiet "phut" rather than an explosive bang. Whatever you do, don't jiggle the bottle wildly, racing-driver style, or the cork will shoot out and you'll lose half the contents.

Have a glass ready and hold it at an angle towards the bottle as you pour (like a beer), so that the bubbles don't cascade over the side. Fill the glass until the bubbles reach the top, then when they have subsided, top up the glass until it is three-quarters full.

★ THE PERFECT GLASS

WHILE CHAMPAGNE WILL TASTE GOOD IN A COFFEE MUG IF THE MOMENT IS RIGHT, THE BEST WAY TO SHOW IT OFF IS TO BUY THE RIGHT SORT OF GLASS. AVOID A FLAT, SAUCER SHAPE, WHICH ALLOWS BOTH THE AROMAS AND BUBBLES TO ESCAPE. INSTEAD, GO FOR A TALL "FLUTE," IDEALLY WITH A BOWL THAT IS SLIGHTLY WIDER IN THE CENTER THAN AT THE RIM, AND WITH A LONG STEM, WHICH YOU CAN HOLD SO YOU DON'T WARM THE GLASS WITH YOUR HAND AS YOU DRINK IT. THE RIM OF THE GLASS SHOULD ALSO BE THIN AND FINE.

IT GOES WITHOUT SAYING THAT YOUR GLASS SHOULD BE CLEAN, BUT IT SHOULD ALSO BE WELL RINSED (DUST AND DETERGENT RESIDUES BOTH BREAK DOWN BUBBLES). DRY THE GLASS WITH A CLEAN, DRY LINEN CLOTH ON WHICH YOU HAVEN'T USED HEAVILY PERFUMED FABRIC SOFTENERS.

how to taste sparkling wine

Tasting a sparkling wine is much like tasting a still one. You want to appreciate the color and aromas as well as the flavors—but there's also the consistency of the bubbles to enjoy.

Pour a little into a glass (page 45), about halfway up the bowl. Look at the color, which may range from light straw to pale gold. Swirl the wine around gently and smell the aromas which waft off the top of the glass. Take a sip and hold it in your mouth, tasting the different flavors and also the texture of the "mousse" (as the bubbles are called). Note how elegant or energetic it is. Does it dance lightly around on your tongue or vigorously bounce off the walls of your palate. Then swallow the wine and see if there's a detectable aftertaste.

Fruit flavors you may notice are citrus (particularly grapefruit and lemon), green apple (in younger wines), peach and nectarine (in riper ones), raspberry and wild strawberry (in rosé champagne), and black currant and cherry in sparkling red wines (see Sparkling Wine Styles pages 30–35).

You may also pick up flavors that are typical of sparkling wine, especially champagne: yeast, freshly baked bread or biscuits, jasmine, almonds, cream, and vanilla, and in older vintages, honey, toasted brioche, grilled hazelnuts, mushrooms, and truffles. Or you might detect a whole spectrum of flavors of your own. Don't be intimidated by what other people find in their glass. Tasting is an entirely personal experience.

Enjoying

Is it possible to enjoy champagne and sparkling wine even more than you do already? Certainly, by treating it as more than just a party drink or what you pour into your glass for a toast.

Sparkling wine is hugely underrated as a partner for food—not just canapés, but all kinds of seafood, salads, white meat, and lightly spiced dishes. It is as flexible as a white wine. Fizz also makes a light, elegant cocktail, less alcoholic than one based on spirits and liqueurs alone.

If you think of sparkling wine in the same way as you think of still wine— that there's a bottle at every price and for every occasion—you will get even more pleasure out of it than you do now.

fizz & food

As any champagne-lover will tell you, fizz is extraordinarily versatile. Its popularity as an aperitif is not simply an accident; sparkling wine actually perks up the palate, stimulating the appetite for food.

The lightness and delicacy of the wine and the playfulness of the bubbles play a major part in the success of sparkling wine and food matches, that would prove otherwise undistinguished with a still wine. The classic combination of champagne and caviar is a fabulous marriage of textures between the exquisite bubbles and the delicate eggs. The same logic applies to foods such as feather-light soufflés, airy meringues, or fragile, wobbly gelatin desserts.

In addition, bubbly is the perfect match for lightly cooked or steamed food, or raw food like salads or sushi, because it doesn't overwhelm the food like some wines can.

Bubbles can also act as a palate cleanser, livening up the smooth unctuous texture of creamy sauces, or providing a refreshing contrast to deep-fried foods or crispy canapés.

Flavor-wise too, there are striking affinities between fizz and certain types of food. Lighter styles of champagne cope perfectly with the saltiness of fresh seafood and the sharpness of fresh fruit like raspberries and rhubarb. Champagne is about the only dry wine you can successfully drink with dessert, while the yeastiness and toastiness of richer styles work perfectly with the *umami* (savory) flavors of roast poultry, mushrooms, and seared food such as scallops.

The type of dishes that don't work so well are Mediterranean-style recipes with cooked tomato sauces and rich meaty sauces, braises, and meat stews. But then what are red wines for?

CLASSIC FIZZ & FOOD COMBINATIONS

Champagne has always been a traditional partner for the finer things in life—luxury
ingredients such as caviar, foie gras, scallops, truffles (white and black), and lobster. However,
you can equally well drink sparkling wine with many simpler foods.

★ **CANAPÉS** All kinds, especially hot, crisp-coated varieties with bread crumbs or gougère (cheese-flavored choux pastry), which is a particularly good match.

★ **RAW AND COLD SHELLFISH** Light, dry styles of fizz go especially well with oysters, fresh crab, shrimp, langoustines, and lobster.

★ **GRILLED OR PAN-FRIED FISH** such as flounder, Dover sole, seabass, or halibut. A simple sauce made from butter, lemon juice, and soft herbs will enhance the experience.

★ **SALMON** Most classic methods of cooking such as broiling or pan-frying work well, but avoid spicy crusts or marinades as they may overwhelm the fizz. Cold poached salmon, smoked salmon (lox), and salmon fishcakes are all fantastic matches.

★ **FISH OR CHICKEN** accompanied with creamy or buttery sauces or sauces made with champagne are delicious served with fizz, as is fish pie.

★ **SIMPLY ROASTED CHICKEN** Choose a more full-bodied style of fizz—vintage if possible. It is fabulous with a really good free-range bird.

★ **RAW AND RARE MEAT** are a good match with fizz, such as carpaccio (thinly sliced raw beef). The Champenois are very keen on the combination of vintage rosé champagne served with rare meat and game, such as lamb cutlets, pigeon, and duck breasts.

★ **MUSHROOMS** have a great affinity with richer, toastier styles of bubbly. They can be served on their own, for example as a wild mushroom tart or risotto, or to enhance a dish with fish or chicken.

★ **LIGHT, MOUSSEY, OR CREAMY FRENCH CHEESES** such as Chaource (appropriately from the Champagne region), Brie, or goat cheese—just don't let them get too sharp. Parmesan is also good.

★ **UNSWEETENED FRESH BERRIES** especially raspberries and strawberries. If you add sugar, cream, or fromage frais, or serve them as a tart, go for a rich or *demi-sec* style champagne.

★ **PEACHES AND NECTARINES** These fruits are both perfect with fizz.

★ **SOUFFLÉS, SPONGE CAKES, AND OTHER LIGHT DESSERTS** Classic French patisserie, such as *millefeuille*, is delicious with medium-dry champagne.

★ IN THE KITCHEN

IT MIGHT SEEM EXTRAVAGANT TO COOK WITH CHAMPAGNE, PARTICULARLY AS THE BUBBLES TEND TO DISAPPEAR WITHIN A COUPLE OF MINUTES, BUT IT CERTAINLY SOUNDS SEXY. IF YOU WANT TO SCHMOOZE (OR SEDUCE) SOMEONE, THERE CAN BE FEW MORE SPECTACULAR WAYS TO DO IT.

YOU CAN SUBSTITUTE CHAMPAGNE (OR SPARKLING WINE) IN ANY RECIPE THAT USES DRY WHITE WINE, SUCH AS CREAMY SAUCES OR RISOTTO. FOR A BASIC CHAMPAGNE SAUCE TO SERVE WITH SALMON OR OYSTERS, FOLLOW THIS SIMPLE METHOD: PUT TWO TABLESPOONS BUTTER IN A SAUCEPAN AND HEAT UNTIL MELTED. ADD A FINELY CHOPPED SHALLOT AND SWEAT IT IN THE BUTTER UNTIL SOFTENED. POUR IN HALF A GLASS OF FIZZ AND SIMMER UNTIL IT HAS REDUCED TO A COUPLE OF TABLESPOONS. ADD AN EQUAL AMOUNT OF HEAVY CREAM, SEASON WITH SEA SALT AND FRESHLY GROUND BLACK PEPPER, AND HEAT UNTIL WARMED THROUGH. IT COULDN'T BE EASIER.

SPARKLING WINE ALSO LENDS ITSELF WELL TO BEING USED IN DESSERTS. IT MAKES FABULOUS JELLOS AND SORBETS, LIGHT AIRY SABAYONS TO SERVE OVER FRUIT AND, BEST OF ALL, AN INSTANT MARINADE FOR FRESH FRUIT—TRY WHITE PEACHES IN PROSECCO. YOU CAN ALSO MAKE CHOCOLATE CHAMPAGNE TRUFFLES, THOUGH I MUST CONFESS I WOULD RATHER LEAVE THIS TO AN EXPERT CHOCOLATIER.

ASIAN FLAVORS

Sparkling wine really comes into its own as a partner to Asian cuisines where the high alcohol levels and oakiness of many modern wines can be overwhelming. Light or *extra brut* champagnes, for example, are extremely good with Japanese raw fish dishes like sushi and sashimi, while rosé champagne is a particularly successful match with raw or seared tuna. Sparkling wine also works well with tofu and tempura. Other good fizz and Asian food matches include:

★ fried and steamed dim sum, especially those based on seafood

★ lighter Cantonese dishes, such as steamed fish and stir-fries

★ clear Asian soups

★ Thai- and Vietnamese-style salads (champagne works particularly well with mint and cilantro)

★ mildly spiced Indian food—again, especially with seafood. Recipes that include turmeric, ginger, and cardamom tend to work well, as do spicy snacks like pakoras and bhajis, provided they're not too hot.

CONTEMPORARY COOKING

Whether you refer to it as Cal Ital, Pan-Asian, Pacific Rim, or Modern British, contemporary menus contain many of the same ingredients and influences. In general, dishes tend to be much lighter than they once were with an emphasis on fresh, simply prepared ingredients. Sparkling wines cope well with this type of cooking—dishes such as goat cheese and asparagus salad, seared seabass with fennel, risotto or pasta with spring vegetables or mushrooms, even a vegetable couscous. Just keep the food light and unfussy.

BRUNCH

Sparkling wine and eggs are a tried and trusted combination. So fizz makes the perfect accompaniment to weekend brunch dishes, such as scrambled eggs and smoked salmon (lox), eggs Benedict, quiche, and kedgeree. Choose a lighter style of fizz, like a Blanc de Blancs champagne or a sparkling Chardonnay.

FAST FOOD AND FIZZ

With the cheapest sparkling wines costing no more than the least expensive still ones, you can afford to pop the cork for take-out treats such as fish—or even fish sticks—and chips, fish tacos, or sneaky snack foods like nachos or tortillas and guacamole. And if you haven't tried a glass of bubbly with popcorn or doughnuts, you haven't lived!

cocktails

It might seem like sacrilege to make cocktails with champagne, but although you can substitute a cheaper sparkling wine perfectly well in most drinks, there is something wonderfully indulgent about using the real thing. Obviously it's a waste to use a hugely expensive vintage champagne or one that you've been saving up for a celebration. What you need is a non-vintage bubbly that's fresh, fruity and—above all—well chilled, as the other ingredients should be, too.

THE CLASSIC CHAMPAGNE COCKTAIL

The dash of ginger does wonders for this great champagne classic.

(MAKES I GLASS)

I SUGAR CUBE OR I TEASPOON SUGAR

A FEW DROPS OF ANGOSTURA BITTERS

2 TEASPOONS BRANDY

ABOUT ½ TEASPOON GINGER-FLAVORED LIQUEUR (OPTIONAL)

WELL-CHILLED CHAMPAGNE

Put the sugar cube or sugar in a glass and sprinkle a few drops of Angostura bitters over it. Add the brandy and ginger liqueur, if using, then slowly top up with well-chilled champagne, tilting the glass towards the bottle as you pour.

SOPHISTICATED COCKTAILS

Feel free to adjust the quantities given depending on the type of fizz you use—you may need a little more or less sugar, for example. If you want to increase the quantities for a party, it's helpful to remember that a champagne glass holds roughly 4 oz. of liquid when three-quarters full.

CHEAT'S CHAMPAGNE COCKTAIL

A party cocktail made with an orange-flavored Cinzano.

(MAKES ABOUT 40 GLASSES)

1 BOTTLE BASIC FRENCH OR SPANISH BRANDY, 750 ML

2 BOTTLES CINZANO ORANCIO, 750 ML EACH

40 DASHES ANGOSTURA BITTERS

5 BOTTLES CAVA, WELL CHILLED

Pour a splash of brandy into each glass and add enough Cinzano Orancio so each glass is just under one-third full. Add a dash of Angostura bitters, and top up with well-chilled cava.

APHRODITE

The classic champagne cocktail with a Greek twist.

(MAKES 1 GLASS)

1 TABLESPOON 5- OR 7-STAR METAXA (GREEK-STYLE BRANDY)

½ TABLESPOON APRICOT BRANDY

A FEW DROPS OF ANGOSTURA BITTERS

WELL-CHILLED CAVA OR OTHER SPARKLING WINE

Pour the Metaxa and apricot brandy into the glass. Add a few drops of Angostura bitters and top up with cava or another inexpensive sparkling wine.

SLOE SPARKLE

With its soft plummy flavor and musky pink color, this is a more subtle version of the classic cocktail Kir Royale, which is made from cassis and champagne.

(MAKES 1 GLASS)

1 TABLESPOON SLOE GIN

WELL-CHILLED CHAMPAGNE OR OTHER SPARKLING WINE

Put the sloe gin in the glass and top up with fizz.

ITALIA 75

This is based on the classic lemon-flavored champagne cocktail known as French 75, but the addition of limoncello gives it an Italian twist.

(MAKES 2 GLASSES)

2 OZ. GIN

1 OZ. FRESHLY SQUEEZED LEMON JUICE

½ OZ. LIMONCELLO OR OTHER LEMON-FLAVORED LIQUEUR

WELL-CHILLED CAVA OR OTHER INEXPENSIVE SPARKLING WINE

Put the gin, lemon juice, and limoncello in a cocktail shaker. Add plenty of ice and shake vigorously. Strain into two champagne glasses and top up with chilled fizz.

BLACK VELVET

This striking combination of stout and champagne sounds unlikely, but it works extraordinarily well, especially with fresh oysters. I prefer Mackeson stout to the traditional Guinness, but use whatever stout you like.

(MAKES ABOUT 10 GLASSES)

2 BOTTLES STOUT, 12 OZ. EACH, WELL CHILLED

1 BOTTLE CHAMPAGNE, 750 ML, WELL CHILLED

Carefully fill the glasses just under half-full with the stout. Slowly top up with the champagne.

SUMMER COCKTAILS

The widespread availability of juicers makes it wonderfully easy to make delicious summery fruit cocktails. My favorite is the Italian Bellini, which is made with Prosecco. All you need for a base is some freshly made fruit juice—you can always add a dash of fruit syrup or fruit liqueur if you feel the fruit you're using is not quite ripe or flavorsome enough.

Using fresh juice seems to make it more likely that your fizz will overflow, so pour it very slowly and carefully, tilting the glass towards the bottle as you pour.

CLASSIC BELLINI

The Bellini was invented at Harry's Bar in Venice. It is traditionally made with white peaches and Prosecco, but you could equally well use yellow peaches and champagne.

(MAKES I GLASS)

ABOUT ¼ CUP FRESHLY MADE WHITE PEACH JUICE (FROM

I LARGE CHILLED PEACH)

WELL-CHILLED PROSECCO OR CHAMPAGNE

2 TEASPOONS PEACH-FLAVORED LIQUEUR, WELL CHILLED (OPTIONAL)

Pour the peach juice to just under halfway up the champagne glass and slowly top up with chilled fizz. Stir carefully and taste, adding a little peach liqueur if you think the peach flavor needs intensifying.

NOTE: You can make a Bellini with many different kinds of freshly juiced fruit: raspberry, strawberry, mixed strawberry and watermelon, and pear are all good. Some fruits are more intense than others—you'll need less raspberry juice, for instance, than you would peach or pear juice. Some fruits, such as peaches and pears, discolor quickly, so use them immediately or add a little lemon juice to stop them turning brown.

FRESH STRAWBERRY SPARKLER

A simple idea, but a very pretty one.

(MAKES 1 GLASS)

1 RIPE MEDIUM STRAWBERRY, HULLED AND THINLY SLICED

A LITTLE SUGAR SYRUP, TO TASTE

WELL-CHILLED ROSÉ CHAMPAGNE OR OTHER PINK SPARKLING WINE

Put the sliced strawberry in the glass, add a dash of sugar syrup to taste, and top up with rosé champagne.

MIMOSA

Bucks fizz with a twist—the ideal drink for an outdoor summer brunch.

(MAKES 8–10 GLASSES)

ABOUT 10 MEDIUM JUICING ORANGES*

8–10 TABLESPOONS GRAND MARNIER OR OTHER

ORANGE-FLAVORED LIQUEUR

ONE 750 ML BOTTLE CHAMPAGNE OR SPARKLING WINE, WELL CHILLED

Squeeze the juice from the oranges and chill it for at least one hour. When ready to serve, put 1 tablespoon Grand Marnier in each glass. Fill each glass just under half-full with the chilled orange juice, then slowly top up with chilled fizz.

*NOTE: You can buy freshly squeezed orange juice instead, but juicing the oranges yourself definitely gives this drink an edge.

FRESH PASSIONFRUIT FIZZ

This makes a romantic cocktail for two.

(MAKES 2 GLASSES)

2 PASSIONFRUIT (CHOOSE ONES WITH SLIGHTLY WRINKLY SKIN)

2–4 TEASPOONS PASSIONFRUIT LIQUEUR, SUCH AS ALIZÉ, OR

PASSIONFRUIT SYRUP

WELL-CHILLED CAVA OR OTHER INEXPENSIVE SPARKLING WINE

Scoop the passionfruit pulp into a small wire mesh strainer and press it through, scraping a knife along the bottom of the strainer to ensure you collect all of it. Spoon it into two chilled glasses, add the passionfruit liqueur or syrup, depending upon how sweet your passionfruit is, and slowly top up with fizz.

SPARKLING SEABREEZE

Although these ingredients are available year-round, this cocktail works particularly well at a summer party.

(MAKES 8–10 GLASSES)

7 OZ. CRANBERRY-FLAVORED VODKA, SUCH AS POLSTAR, CHILLED

1 CUP GRAPEFRUIT JUICE, CHILLED (USE PINK GRAPEFRUIT JUICE IF

YOUR VODKA IS COLORLESS)

1 BOTTLE SPARKLING WINE OR CHAMPAGNE, 750 ML, WELL CHILLED

Put the cranberry vodka and grapefruit juice in a large pitcher and mix well. Add the sparkling wine, stir gently, then slowly pour into the glasses.

glossary

ASSEMBLAGE The blend of wines that forms the basis of the final champagne

BLANC DE BLANCS A champagne made exclusively from light-skinned grapes, that is to say, Chardonnay

BLANC DE NOIRS A champagne made exclusively from dark-skinned grapes—Pinot Noir and Pinot Meunier

BRUT Describes a champagne that is dry, but which, in practice, always has a little sugar added (the equivalent German term is *trocken*)

CAVE A champagne cellar

CUVÉE A particular bottling. Prestige cuvée is the name a champagne producer gives to his top wine

DEMI-SEC Half-dry, or medium-dry. Best drunk as a dessert champagne

DOSAGE The sweetened wine added to top up the champagne bottle and to correct the sweetness after the yeast residue is removed

EXTRA BRUT A champagne with no added sugar, also known as *brut nature* and *ultra brut*

GRAND CRU The highest-ranked villages and vineyards in Champagne

GRANDE MARQUE A top producer—literally "a great brand"

MOUSSE The consistency of the bubbles, as in "a fine mousse"

NON-VINTAGE A champagne that is blended from wines from more than one harvest

PREMIER CRU The second-highest ranked villages and vineyards in the Champagne region

RICH Increasingly popular style—slightly drier than *demi-sec*. Commonly drunk with foie gras and mildly spiced Thai, Chinese, or other Asian food

SEC Should mean "dry," but it is in fact fairly sweet. Quite rare nowadays

VINTAGE A champagne made from wines from a single harvest

how to read a champagne label

MAILLY BLANC DE NOIRS

FONDÉ EN 1929: the date when the co-operative was founded

CHAMPAGNE: indicates the producer has the right to use the Champagne name

MAILLY: the name of the producer

GRAND CRU: the village's vineyards are classified as Grand Cru—the best in the Champagne region

BLANC DE NOIRS: indicates the wine is made from only the dark-skinned Pinot Noir and Pinot Meunier grapes, that is to say there's no Chardonnay used. This gives it a particularly full, rich flavor

750 ML: the amount of wine in the bottle

BRUT: dry, with a minimal amount of sugar added

12% VOL: the percentage by volume of alcohol in the wine

ELABORÉE PAR LA SOCIÉTÉ DE PRODUCTEURS 51500, MAILLY: shows the wine comes from a co-operative of growers, not a single house

If there is no date on the bottle, this indicates that the champagne is non-vintage, that is to say that it is blended from grapes from different harvests

You may also find the following initials on champagne bottles:

NM: meaning *négociant manipulant*—an organization that buys grapes or juice and turns it into champagne. The big champagne houses come into this category

CM: *co-opérative manipulant*—a growers' co-operative

RM: *récoltant manipulant*—a grower who produces his/her own champagne as opposed to selling the grapes to another producer

further information

If you want to find out more about champagne and sparkling wine, log on to:

www.champagne.fr
The official website of the Comité Interprofessionnel du Vin de Champagne (C.I.V.C.), the official body which regulates the champagne industry.

www.umc.fr
The website of the *grandes marques*, the big champagne houses. Lists producers whose cellars you can visit.

www.champagnemagic.com
The champagne enthusiast's website, with a comprehensive list of producers.

www.aube-champagne.com
Tourist guide to this little-known part of the region.

www.crcava.es
All you need to know about cava . . .

www.prosecco.it
. . . and Prosecco.

www.winecountry.com
A comprehensive guide to touring the wine regions of California. Links to sparkling wine producers.

www.winediva.com.au
Australian wine site with links to 221 sparkling wine producers and information about local wine tourism.

www.decanter.com and
www.winespectactor.com
The on-line versions of the top English and American wine magazines. Includes features on and tastings of champagne and other sparkling wines.

www.wine-pages.com
Excellent e-magazine, which has champagne expert Tom Stevenson (below) as a contributor.

Further reading:
Champagne enthusiasts should get hold of *Christie's World Encyclopedia of Champagne & Sparkling Wine* by Tom Stevenson ($50.00, Wine Appreciation Guild).

credits

Many thanks to the C.I.V.C. for supplying me with up-to-date information about the Champagne region and to Duval-Leroy, Jacquesson, Mailly, Moët et Chandon, Pol Roger, Louis Roederer, and Vilmart who welcomed me at their cellars. Thanks, too, to Patrick Materman, senior winemaker for Montana of New Zealand, for his expertise. And last but not least, to the highly professional team at Ryland Peters & Small—Alison Starling, Sharon Ashman, Pamela Daniels, and Steve Painter.

For Trevor, who shares most of the bottles of fizz I open.
Thank you for everything.

picture credits

Key: ph= photographer, a=above, b=below, r=right, l=left, c=center

All photographs by Peter Cassidy unless otherwise stated.

Page 5 ph Ian Wallace; 7 & 8 ph William Lingwood; 9r, 10, & 11 © ph Alan Williams; 12–13a © ph Alan Williams; 12–13b courtesy of Taittinger; 14a ph Alan Williams; 14b courtesy of Taittinger; 17 courtesy of Taittinger; 18–19b & 20 ph Alan Williams; 21r © Freixenet; 22 both © RidgeView Wine Estate; 23 ph Ian Wallace; 24l ph Alan Williams; 30 background ph Alan Williams; 32ar ph William Lingwood; 32br courtesy of Taittinger; 42al & ar courtesy of Taittinger; 42bl © Freixenet; 45 inset ph Caroline Arber; 47 all insets ph Francesca Yorke; 53r courtesy of Champagne Jacquart, Reims, France; 54ar & 55ar ph Alan Williams; 56–59 ph William Lingwood; 60a & 60–61c ph William Lingwood; 60–61b courtesy of Taittinger; 62–63 & 64 ph Alan Williams.

The publisher would like to thank Hatch Mansfield, R&R Teamwork, Freixenet, RidgeView Wine, and Emma Wellings PR for providing pictures from the following wine producers:

Champagne Jacquart, France

Taittinger, France

Freixenet, Spain

RidgeView Wine Estate, England

index

CONVERSION CHART

Measures have been rounded up or down slightly to make measuring easier.

IMPERIAL	METRIC
½ oz.	12.5 ml
1 oz. (single)	25 ml
2 oz. (double)	50 ml
3 oz.	75 ml
4 oz.	100 ml
5 oz.	125 ml
6 oz.	150 ml
7 oz.	175 ml
8 oz.	200 ml